Low Fat

BARNES
&NOBLE
BOOKS
NEW YORK

Contents

Low-fat Cooking
Typical ingredients

If your trousers or skirt feel tight and the scales indicate slightly more than you like, then there's only one thing to do: Shed some of those excess pounds! It's estimated that every third adult has a weight problem—and more and more children are going the same way. Why? Because we're eating too much—especially fat.

A combination of fast food—which we all know is far from healthy—and a lack of exercise means that a substantial amount of what we eat goes straight to the abdomen, bottom, and hips. Fat makes us fat; it contains almost twice as many calories as the same amount of protein or carbohydrate. To lose weight, we have to apply the "fat brakes." We consume about 4½ ounces of fat every day, yet our metabolism needs only between 2 and 3 ounces to function efficiently. Piling our plates with more carbohydrates from cereals, pasta, potatoes, fruit, and vegetables, reducing visible fat, becoming wise to "hidden fats," and learning to avoid them—these are the principles of low-fat cooking. And because practically nothing is banned (as long as you choose the low-fat option), you won't feel you're missing out.

FRUIT: Fresh fruit (left) is naturally virtually fat-free. It also contains wonderful combinations of energizing vitamins, easy-to-digest fruit sugars (fructose), and lots of essential water.

1 MILK PRODUCTS AND CHEESE: Cottage cheese, yogurt, and low-fat cheese are all excellent sources of calcium. Go for the low fat or fat-free option; use coffee creamer (10% fat) instead of cream, and always read the label when buying cheese. A general rule of thumb is the creamier the cheese, the higher its fat content.

2 POTATOES: This healthy source of carbohydrate is extremely versatile and always a hit—whether in the form of soup, a silky-smooth mash that needs no cream or butter at all, or baked in its skin and served with a light dip.

3 VEGETABLES AND LEGUMES: Root, leaf, and tuberous vegetables are bursting with minerals, trace elements, vitamins, and vitalizing bio materials, secondary plant materials. Soy products and legumes are excellent sources of protein. Vegetables and legumes contain hardly any fat at all, but lots of fiber, which fills us up and keeps the digestive system fit and happy.

4 FISH: Low-fat varieties include all white fish such as snapper, monkfish, and cod; halibut, salmon, herring and eel—especially the latter—are oilier. However, because saltwater fish contains lots of iodine and essential unsaturated fatty acids, you really can eat as much as you like.

5 HERBS: Virtually no fat or calories. They add freshness and flavor and are a good substitute for salt and the flavor-carrier fat.

6 HIGH QUALITY VEGETABLE OILS: If you're going to eat fat, then make sure it's the right kind. Our bodies need fat to absorb the fat-soluble vitamins A, D, E, and K from our food. Unlike animal fats, plant-based oils provide essential fatty acids. Cold-pressed oils made from olives and sunflower seeds are highly recommended.

7 NUTS AND SEEDS: They contain lots of vitamin E, but because of their high fat content they should be eaten only in small quantities.

CEREALS AND WHOLE-GRAIN PRODUCTS: Rice, corn, wheat, and other cereals are high-quality, plant-based sources of protein. Whole-grain products instantly boost your intake of vitamins and trace elements.

MEAT: Choose low-fat varieties, such as chicken, turkey, game, and lean beef, and low-fat cuts, such as tenderloin and flank. Remove all visible fat—including that on sliced or cured ham.

How to Use Less Fat
Tips and hints

Cutting down on fat actually starts before you even go shopping. You need to know how much fat different foods contain so that you can avoid them and eat healthily and "low fat" in the long term. However, there's more to healthy eating than simply knowing all about low-fat foods and choosing them—plenty of "fat traps" still lurk in the kitchen and we need to know how to avoid them too.

Using less fat is child's play with the right tools: You'll be making more use of steamers, nonstick pots and pans, woks, chicken bricks, foil, roasting bags, and nonstick baking parchment in the future. By using this equipment and the appropriate cooking methods you'll be able to use the minimum amount of fat. Get used to measuring even small amounts; don't just pour oil lavishly into the pan, and use a teaspoon or spray to distribute it evenly over a salad. Replace foods that have a very high fat content with reduced-fat options whenever you can, such as low-fat yogurt instead of crème fraîche. As well as trimming off fat before you cook, you can also remove some from many dishes after cooking. Drain deep-fried food on paper towels and scoop off the oil floating on top of soups or sauces.

Cooking methods that use less fat

1 Fish and vegetables are excellent steamed in a bamboo basket, metal steamer, or cooked in a pressure cooker.

2 Let vegetables, meat, and fish simmer in their own juices. Use a pot or chicken brick, or wrap in foil or nonstick parchment.

3 Stir frying in a wok is quick, requires very little fat, and retains the color, texture, and flavor of the ingredients.

4 Whether over charcoal or under a conventional broiler—broiling adds flavor and is a virtually fat-free technique.

▶▶ You will find the calories (kcal) and fat content (g fat) at the end of the list of ingredients in the recipes. The information given is per person.

Where the fat is

Dairy products	grams of fat per 100g
Mascarpone	48
Crème fraîche	40
Cream	32
Whole milk cream cheese	11
Sour cream	10
Coffee creamer (10% fat)	10
Coffee creamer (4% fat)	4
Whole milk yogurt	3.5
Whole milk	3.5
Cottage cheese	3
Low-fat yogurt	1.5
Low-fat milk	1.5
Buttermilk	0.5
Low-fat farmer's cheese	0.3
Skim milk	0.3
Skim yogurt	0.1
Hen's egg	12

Cheese	grams of fat per 100g
Blue cheese	40
Cheddar	34
Swiss cheese	33
Gorgonzola	31
Emmenthal	30
Roquefort	40
Whole milk soft cheese	28
Brie	26
Parmesan	26
Edam	25
Gouda	22
Goat cheese	22
Camembert	22
Feta	19
Lindenberger	18
Mozzarella	16
Low-fat Cheddar	15
Ricotta	11
Soft cheese	8

Fish and shellfish	grams of fat per 100g
Eel	25
Herring	18
Tuna	16
Salmon	14
Mackerel	12
Sardine	5
Swordfish	4
Porgy	4
Trout	3
Flounder	2
Catfish	2
Crab	2
Shrimp	1
Mussels	1
Cod	1
Clams	1
Squid	1
Haddock	1
Abalone	0.5

Meat, poultry, game	grams of fat per 100g
Pork shoulder	20
Duck	17
Beef chuck or blade	16
Chicken leg (skin on)	11
Chicken leg (skin off)	8
Lamb chop (trimmed)	8
Port chop (trimmed)	8
Venison	6
Roast beef	4
Beef tenderloin	4
Turkey leg (skin off)	4
Rabbit	4
Lamb fillet	3
Veal knuckle steak	2
Veal scallop	2
Pork tenderloin	2
Pork scallop (skin off)	2
Chicken breast portion (skin off)	1
Turkey scallop	1

Cold cuts	grams of fat per 100g
Fatty bacon	65
Smoked ham (untrimmed)	35
Cervelat	35
Salami	33
Mortadella	33
Bolony	33
Liverwurst	29
Wiener	28
Meat loaf	28
Gelbwurst	27
Frankfurter	24
Garlic sausage	19
Polish sausage	18
Lean bacon	14
Cooked ham	13
Bierschinken	11
Corned beef	7
Lean pork (trimmed)	3
Roast turkey breast	2

Cakes and snacks	grams of fat per 100g
Roasted peanuts	50
Potato chips	40
Peanut snacks	36
Chocolate bar	30
Milk chocolate	30
Nut snack bar	28
Marzipan	25
Popcorn	20
Cream cake	20
Danish	18
Mud cake	16
Key lime pie	14
Jelly roll with fruit cream	10
Cheesecake	8
Apple strudel	5
Tray bake (yeast based) with fruit topping	4
Japanese rice cakes	2
Pretzel	1

Snacks & Soups

Beet Mousse
with Horseradish

Quick to prepare and totally irresistible: This delicious mousse
is a delight—to look at and to eat

Ingredients

12 ounces **beet**

generous 1 cup **farmer's cheese**

small piece of fresh **horseradish**

¼ cup **crème fraîche**

or **sour cream**

salt · pepper

1 tablespoon **balsamic vinegar**

¾ ounce **Romano cheese** (piece)

⏵⏵ 175 kcal, 10 g fat

Preparation
SERVES 4

1 Wash and trim the beet but do not peel. Reserve a few leaves for the garnish if you like. Cook the beet in a little boiling water for 40 minutes. Drain, plunge into cold water, drain, and peel (wear latex gloves to avoid staining your hands.)

2 Coarsely grate about one-third of the cooked beet. Place the remainder in a blender with the farmer's cheese and process until completely smooth.

3 Peel the horseradish, grate finely, and combine it and the crème fraîche with the beet mousse. Season to taste with salt, pepper, and balsamic vinegar.

4 Arrange the beet mousse and grated beet in small serving dishes. Grate over the Romano cheese and garnish with a few beet leaves if you like. Serve with rustic bread.

This mousse is easier and quicker to prepare if you use precooked beet or baby beets, sealed in vacuum packs, and available from most good supermarkets.

Green Vegetables
with Tuna Sauce

Preparation
SERVES 4

1 Wash and trim the vegetables. Peel the lower third of the asparagus and trim the ends. Cut the zucchini lengthwise into four pieces. Cut the celery stalks in half lengthwise, and then cut everything into 4-inch long pieces. Trim the beans and snow peas, but leave whole.

2 Season the vegetables with salt and pepper and sprinkle over the lime rind. Steam over boiling water until just tender, but still firm to the bite.

3 To make the sauce, pour the contents of the can of tuna into a blender, add the sour cream and lime juice, and process until smooth.

4 Wash the parsley and shake dry. Pull off the leaves from the stalks and chop finely. Stir the parsley and the capers into the sauce, season well with salt and pepper, and serve with the steamed vegetables. Fresh Italian bread is a good accompaniment.

14

Ingredients

3¼ pounds **mixed vegetables**

(such as asparagus, zucchini, celery, beans, scallions, snow peas)

grated rind and juice of 1 **lime**

salt · pepper

5 ounces canned **tuna** in water

(drained weight)

2 tablespoons **sour cream**

½ bunch of **parsley**

2 tablespoons small **capers**

173 kcal, 7 g fat

Ingredients

3 tablespoons peeled **almonds**

⅔ cup **whole milk plain yogurt**

1 tablespoon **lemon juice**

¼ teaspoon **sea salt**

pepper

½ bunch of fresh **lemon balm**

11 ounces **carrots**

1 **apple**

▸▸ **112 kcal, 6 g fat**

Carrot Salad
with Lemon Balm

Preparation
SERVES 4

1 To make the salad dressing, finely grind 2 tablespoons of the almonds, then whisk with the yogurt, lemon juice, salt, and a little pepper in a bowl, using a balloon whisk.

2 Wash and shake dry the lemon balm and pull off the leaves from the stalks. Reserve a few leaves for the garnish, then finely chop or slice the remainder, and stir into the salad dressing.

3 Trim and peel the carrots, then grate coarsely, and combine with the salad dressing. Wash and halve the apple and remove the core. Peel it if you like, then grate coarsely, and add to the salad.

4 Chop the remaining almonds. Roast in a dry, nonstick skillet until golden, then sprinkle over the salad. Garnish with lemon balm and serve immediately. Do not make this salad much in advance or the apple will discolor.

Asparagus Salad
with Rolled Roast Beef

A special kind of spring greeting: Delicate asparagus, elegant roast beef, and crunchy radishes are enough to make any gastronome's heart beat a little faster

Ingredients

2¾ pounds asparagus · salt

1 tablespoon butter

3 tablespoons lemon juice

sugar · 1 bunch of radishes

1 apple · 1 bunch of scallions

1 tablespoon fruit vinegar

1 tablespoon mustard · pepper

1 tablespoon apple juice

2 tablespoons oil

1 bunch of fresh chives

5 ounces roast beef (sliced)

▶▶ **222 kcal, 10 g fat**

Preparation
SERVES 4

1 Peel the asparagus and trim off any tough stalks. Add a pinch of salt, the butter, 1 tablespoon of the lemon juice, and a large pinch of sugar to a large pan of water and bring to a boil. Add the asparagus and cook for 15–18 minutes.

2 Trim and wash the radishes and cut into fourths. Wash and halve the apple, core, and slice thinly. Trim and wash the scallions and slice diagonally.

3 To make the dressing, combine the remaining lemon juice, the vinegar, mustard, salt, pepper, and apple juice in a small bowl, then whisk in the oil.

4 Wash the chives and shake dry, then slice them. Drain the asparagus and let cool slightly. Cut the stalks in half diagonally, then arrange on individual plates with the radishes, apple, and scallions. Roll up the slices of roast beef and add to the plates.

5 Sprinkle the dressing over the salad, adding a little pumpkin seed oil if you like, and garnish with the chives. Serve with fresh bread.

Aromatic oils, such as pumpkin seed, walnut, or hazelnut oil, add a lovely finishing touch to many salads. Decant into a spray or pump-action bottle to keep the amount you use to a minimum.

Shrimp
Wrapped in Leeks

Asian finger food: Served hot or lukewarm, these delightful shrimp skewers will be a success at any buffet

Ingredients

8 raw jumbo shrimp

2 leeks · salt · 2 garlic cloves

½-inch piece of fresh

ginger root

½ bunch of fresh parsley

1 tablespoon honey

juice of 1 lemon

4 tablespoons dry sherry

4 tablespoons sesame oil

pepper

1 tablespoon sesame seeds

170 kcal, 7 g fat

Preparation
SERVES 4

1 Peel the shrimp, cut along the back, and remove the dark vein that runs along it. Rinse under cold water and pat dry.

2 Trim the leeks, then cut lengthwise, and wash thoroughly. Select eight unblemished leaves and blanch briefly in lightly salted, boiling water, then plunge into ice water, and drain.

3 To make the marinade, peel and finely chop the garlic and ginger. Wash the parsley and shake dry, then pull the leaves off the stalks, and chop finely. Combine the garlic, ginger, parsley, honey, lemon juice, sherry, and 3 tablespoons of the sesame oil in a shallow dish, then season with salt and pepper. Add the shrimp and marinate for about 20 minutes.

4 Remove the shrimp from the marinade and drain on paper towels. Wrap a piece of leek around each one and secure in place with a skewer.

5 Heat the remaining sesame oil in a skillet and cook the shrimp on all sides for about 5 minutes. Sprinkle over the sesame seeds, then remove the shrimp from the skillet. If you like, you could arrange the shrimp on slices of lime before serving.

Oil is essential for marinades because it carries the flavor. The marinated ingredients have so much flavor that it is not really necessary to use any more of the marinade during cooking.

Winter Salad Greens
with Herbs and Cheese

Preparation
SERVES 4

1 Trim the green vegetables, then rinse, and cut into bitesize pieces. Blanch each variety in turn in lightly salted, boiling water. Remove with a slotted spoon, plunge into ice water, and drain.

2 Trim and wash the fennel bulbs, cut them in half lengthwise, and then cut crosswise into thin slices. Pick over the arugula and herbs, then wash and shake dry. Trim, wash, and chop the scallions. Crumble the Roquefort between your fingers.

3 Melt the butter in a skillet, then briefly cook the green vegetables and fennel for 1–2 minutes, until tender-crisp, before seasoning with salt and pepper. Arrange in bowls with the arugula and herbs.

4 Dice the lemon slices and sauté briefly in the skillet. Pour in the stock, then add the olive oil, stirring well, and season with salt and pepper. Add the scallions, then pour the sauce over the salad. Top with the crumbled Roquefort before serving.

Ingredients

2¼ pounds **green vegetables** (such as broccoli flowerets, beans, spinach, zucchini, and snow peas)

salt · 2 **fennel bulbs** · 2 bunches of **arugula**

fresh herbs (such as parsley, tarragon, and chervil)

2 **scallions** · 3 ounces **Roquefort cheese**

2 **lemon slices** · 1 tablespoon **butter**

pepper · 4 tablespoons **vegetable stock**

2 tablespoons **olive oil**

▶▶ **209 kcal, 11 g fat**

Ingredients

9 ounces mealy **potatoes**

1 tablespoon **pine nuts**

8–10 fresh **basil sprigs**

generous ½ cup **soft buttermilk cheese**

salt · white pepper

1 **egg white**

¼ cup **heavy cream**

1¼ pounds small **tomatoes**

1 tablespoon **balsamic vinegar**

1 tablespoon **olive oil**

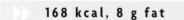 **168 kcal, 8 g fat**

Basil Gnocchi
on Sliced Tomatoes

Preparation
SERVES 4

1 Wash the potatoes, then cook, covered, in lightly salted, boiling water for 20–25 minutes. Roast the pine nuts in a dry, nonstick skillet until golden. Wash the basil and shake dry. Set a few leaves aside for the garnish and finely chop the remainder.

2 Drain the potatoes, then peel. Press through a potato ricer or mash well while still warm. Combine with the pine nuts, chopped basil, and soft cheese.

3 Season and let cool. Beat the egg white until stiff and whip the cream separately, then combine with the basil and potato mixture. Cover and chill for 2 hours.

4 Trim and wash the tomatoes, then slice, and arrange on plates. Season with salt and pepper and sprinkle over the vinegar and oil. Dip two tablespoons in water and scoop gnocchi out of the basil mixture. Arrange on the tomato slices and garnish with basil leaves before serving.

Rice Paper Parcels
with a Mango Filling

Deliciously Asian: The filling inside these exotic parcels
combines the sweetness of juicy mangoes with the spiciness of chile

Ingredients

1 tablespoon **peanut oil**

½ cup **risotto rice**

(arborio or Vialone)

1¼ cups **vegetable stock** · salt

4 **scallions**

1 **lime**

1 fresh **red chile**

1 **mango**

12 sheets of **rice paper**

(about 6½ inches square)

201 kcal, 3 g fat

Preparation
SERVES 4

1 Heat the oil in a pan, then stir in the rice, and cook for 1–2 minutes, until translucent. Pour in the stock and season with salt. Cover and simmer gently over low heat for about 25 minutes.

2 Trim the scallions, rinse, and chop . Wash the lime in hot water, dry, then grate the rind, and squeeze the juice. Cut the chile in half lengthwise, seed, rinse, and finely chop the flesh.

3 Combine 2 tablespoons of the scallions and 2 tablespoons of the lime juice with a little of the chile and set aside. Stir the remaining scallions, chile, and lime juice into the rice.

4 Peel the mango and cut the flesh from the large, central pit. Cut about half into slices and set aside. Finely chop the remainder and stir into the rice.

5 Spread out the rice paper on damp dishtowels, sprinkle with water, and cover with more damp dishtowels. Leave the rice paper to soften for 10–15 minutes.

6 Place a generous tablespoon of the rice mixture on each sheet of rice paper, then fold in the sides to make neat parcels, and tie up with blanched sliced leeks if you like. Arrange on plates with the sliced mango and sprinkle over a little of the scallion and lime juice sauce. Serve the remaining sauce separately.

Cold Cucumber Soup
with Dill Sprigs

Something to **energize** you: A chilled, refreshing soup at the end of a
hot day revitalizes, and provides a **welcome** burst of minerals

Ingredients

1 cucumber

1 garlic clove

1¼ cups vegetable stock

scant ½ cup farmer's cheese

1¾ cups whole milk plain yogurt

salt · pepper

2 eggs · 2 pickled gherkins

½ bunch of fresh dill

▶▶ **160 kcal, 8 g fat**

Preparation
SERVES 4

1 Peel the cucumber and cut in half lengthwise. Scoop out the seeds with a teaspoon, then slice the flesh.

2 Peel and finely chop the garlic. Put in a blender with the cucumber slices, stock, farmer's cheese, and yogurt and process until smooth. Season well with salt and pepper and pour into a bowl.

3 Boil the eggs for about 8 minutes until hard. Drain, plunge into cold water, and shell. Finely chop the eggs and gherkins, then stir them into the soup. Cover and chill.

4 Wash the dill and shake dry. Reserve a few sprigs for the garnish and finely chop the remainder.

5 Stir the chopped dill into the soup and ladle it into chilled bowls. Garnish with reserved dill sprigs and sliced cucumber if you like.

This soup may be served with croûtons instead of chopped egg. Toast two slices of whole-wheat bread, then sauté in melted butter, turning frequently, until golden and crisp. Cut into squares.

Vegetable Soup
with Arugula Pesto

Popular with our Italian neighbors: Pesto gives this otherwise
fairly ordinary soup an aromatic kick

Ingredients

5 ounces **arugula leaves**

2 tablespoons **pine nuts**

2 **garlic cloves** · ¼ cup **olive oil**

3½ cups **vegetable stock**

salt · **pepper**

3 tablespoons freshly grated

Parmesan cheese

5 ounces each **potatoes**,

kohlrabi, carrots, and **snow peas**

3 tablespoons **dry sherry**

233 kcal, 10 g fat

Preparation
SERVES 2

1 Trim and wash the arugula leaves, then dry in a salad spinner or
shake dry. Combine half the arugula with the pine nuts, peeled
garlic, 3 tablespoons of the olive oil, and 3 tablespoons of the
stock in a blender and process until smooth. Scrape into a bowl,
season with salt and pepper, and add the Parmesan.

2 Trim and rinse the potatoes, kohlrabi, and carrots and chop
into small dice. Trim and rinse the snow peas and cut in half
diagonally. Tear the remaining arugula leaves into pieces.

3 Heat the remaining oil in a heavy pan and cook the diced
potatoes, kohlrabi, and carrots. Pour in the remaining stock,
cover, and cook for about 10 minutes. Add the snow peas and
cook for 2 minutes more. Season with salt and pepper to taste
and stir in the sherry.

4 Ladle the soup into bowls and garnish with arugula leaves.
Serve the arugula pesto separately.

**Dandelion leaves can also be used for this recipe,
which will give the pesto a slightly less peppery
taste. Make sure that you pick pesticide- and
pollution-free dandelion leaves. They are
seasonal, so they may not always be available.**

Arabian Summer Soup
with Chicken

A touch of 1001 Nights: Lemon juice adds an incomparable freshness to this exotic green vegetable soup

Ingredients

14 ounces fresh **leafy greens**

(such as spinach, beet greens,

bok choy)

salt · 4 cups **vegetable stock**

1 **chicken breast** portion

1 **onion** · 2 **garlic cloves**

1 **carrot** · 2 **celery stalks**

1 tablespoon **clarified butter**

(or half oil and half butter)

pepper

2–3 tablespoons **lemon juice**

1 teaspoon grated **lemon rind**

160 kcal, 4 g fat

Preparation
SERVES 4

1 Trim and wash the greens and blanch in lightly salted, boiling water. Drain, then plunge into cold water, and drain well.

2 Bring the stock to a boil in a large pan. Rinse the chicken and pat dry, add to the stock, and simmer gently for 10 minutes. Remove the chicken from the stock, cool, then chill. Push the stock through a fine strainer into a bowl.

3 Peel and finely chop the onion and garlic. Trim and peel the carrot. Trim and wash the celery. Cut the carrot and celery into julienne strips.

4 Melt the clarified butter in a pan or heat the oil and butter. Add the onion, garlic, carrot, and celery and cook over medium heat, stirring occasionally, until softened and glazed. Lower the heat, pour in the stock, and heat gently, but do not let boil. Simmer for about 20 minutes.

5 Skin the chicken, then remove the flesh from the bones, and cut into thin strips. Stir into the stock with the blanched greens, season with salt, pepper, lemon juice, and lemon rind, and serve.

6 If you like, cut a slice of bread into cubes. Melt 1 teaspoon of clarified butter in a nonstick skillet, fry the bread until crisp, and sprinkle over the soup.

Fish & Meat

Fisherman's Stew
with Fish and Shellfish

Dip in and enjoy: Everything from the day's catch goes into this wonderful dish—there's even a lobster

Ingredients

2 onions · 4 garlic cloves

1 red and 1 green fresh chile

4 tomatoes

3 tablespoons olive oil

1 cup tomato paste

1½ cups white wine

2 fresh oregano sprigs · salt

pepper · 1¼ pounds mussels

1¼ pounds sea bass fillet

1 tablespoon lemon juice

1 cooked lobster (1¼ pounds)

½ bunch of fresh parsley

315 kcal, 5 g fat

Preparation
SERVES 4

1 Peel and finely chop the onions and garlic. Halve and seed the chiles, then rinse, and finely chop the flesh. Place the tomatoes in a bowl, add boiling water to cover, and let stand for 2 minutes. Drain the tomatoes, peel, halve, and seed.

2 Heat the oil in a large pan and cook the onions, garlic, and chile until softened. Stir the tomato paste into the wine and add to the pan with the tomato halves.

3 Wash the oregano and shake dry, pull off the leaves, and add to the tomato mixture. Season well with salt and pepper, then cover, and simmer gently for about 15 minutes.

4 Scrub the mussels and scrape off any "beards." Discard any mussels with damaged shells or that do not shut immediately when sharply tapped. Wash the fish fillet, cut it into chunks, and sprinkle with lemon juice. Cut the lobster in half lengthwise, remove and discard the stomach sac, and scoop out the flesh. Crack the claws with a hammer and scoop out the flesh. Cut the flesh into chunks. Add the fish, mussels, and lobster to the sauce and simmer gently for 7 minutes.

5 Meanwhile, wash the parsley and shake dry. Pull off the leaves from the stalks and chop finely. Sprinkle the parsley over the stew and serve immediately.

Halibut
in Paper Parcels

The secret's in the wrapping: Thin paper protects the delicate
fish from the heat and retains the wonderful aroma

Ingredients

2 small **leeks**

10 **pimiento-stuffed olives**

4 **garlic cloves**

16 fresh **thyme sprigs**

4 **lemons**

about 4 tablespoons **oil**

salt

pepper

4 **halibut fillets**

267 kcal, 10 g fat

Preparation
SERVES 4

1 Preheat the oven to 400°F. Trim the leeks, rinse, and cut into
2-inch strips. Slice the olives. Peel and halve the garlic.

2 Wash the thyme and shake dry, then shred slightly. Wash
two of the lemons in hot water and cut them into wedges.
Squeeze the juice from the other two lemons. To make the
dressing, combine 4 tablespoons lemon juice with 2 tablespoons
oil and season with salt and pepper.

3 Take eight sheets of wax paper (each about 8 x 12 inches) and
place in pairs, one on top of the other. Lightly oil the centers.
Divide the strips of leek among the sheets of paper and season
with salt and pepper. Rinse the halibut fillets and pat dry with
paper towels. Place one on each piece of paper and sprinkle with
the dressing. Place the olives, thyme, lemon wedges, and garlic on
top of the fish. Fold the paper over the fish and fold down the
top to secure.

4 Lightly oil an ovenproof dish and arrange the parcels inside. Bake
for about 20 minutes. Open the parcels to serve.

**Aluminum foil, roasting bags, and baking
parchment may also be used for this
recipe instead of wax paper. Slices of
tomato or zucchini would add extra
succulence to the dish.**

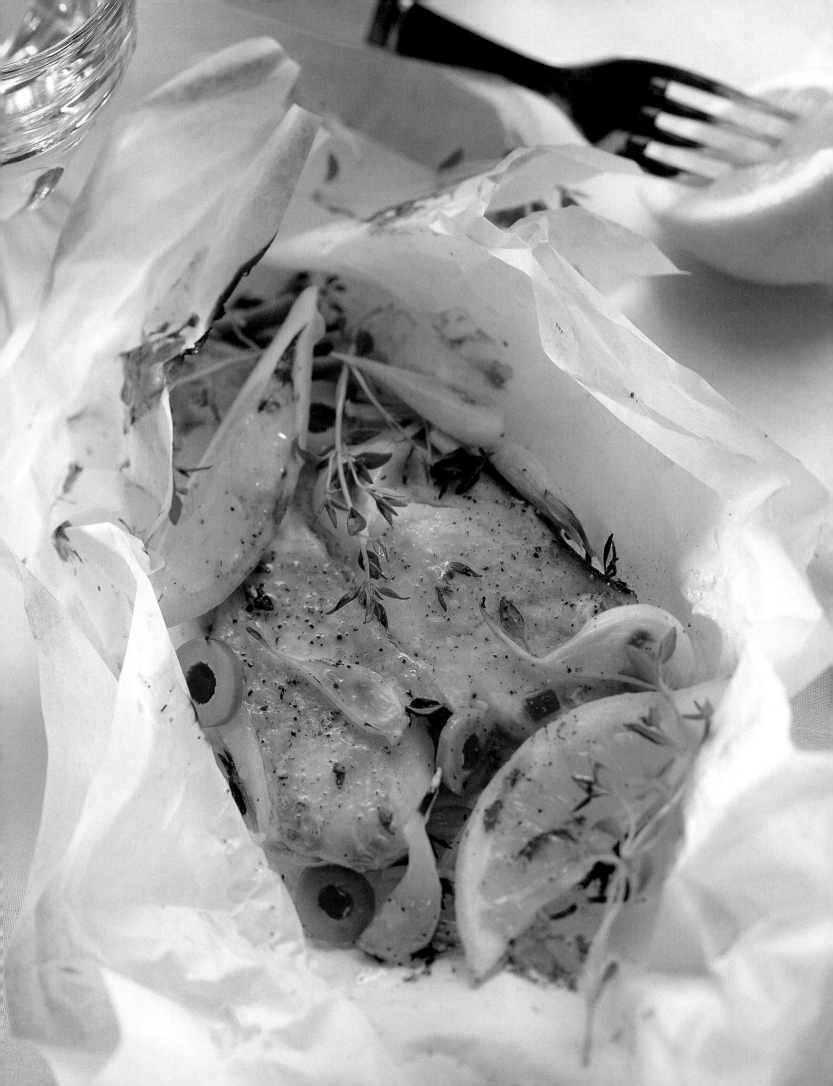

Whiting Fillets
with Celery and Orange

Preparation
SERVES 4

1 Wash the fish and pat dry with paper towels. Season with salt and pepper and sprinkle with the lemon juice. Trim and rinse the celery. Reserve a few of the green leaves for the garnish. Cut the stalks into ½-inch pieces.

2 Peel the oranges with a sharp knife, taking care to remove all the bitter, white pith. Cut the segments from between the membranes, working over a bowl to catch the juice. Squeeze the juice from the membranes into the bowl.

3 Blanch the celery in lightly salted, boiling water for 5 minutes, then drain, and plunge into ice water.

4 Melt the butter in a skillet and cook the fish for about 3 minutes on each side, then remove, and keep warm.

5 Pour the oil and orange juice into the skillet and simmer gently. Heat the celery in the juices, then season with salt and pepper. Arrange the fish fillets and celery with the orange segments and garnish with the celery leaves.

Ingredients

4 **whiting fillets** (each 9 ounces)

salt

pepper

2 tablespoons **lemon juice**

8 **celery stalks** · 4 **oranges**

¼ cup **butter**

2 tablespoons **olive oil**

▷▷ **365 kcal, 8 g fat**

Ingredients

1¼ pounds **green asparagus**

11 ounces **smoked salmon**

salt · 14 ounces dried **tagliolini**

1 tablespoon **olive oil**

pepper

4 tablespoons **lemon juice**

2 tablespoons finely grated **lemon rind**

▶▶ **600 kcal, 16 g fat**

Tagliolini
with Salmon and Asparagus

Preparation
SERVES 4

1 Wash the asparagus, peel the lower third, and cut the stems into chunks. Thinly slice the smoked salmon.

2 Cook the asparagus in lightly salted, boiling water for about 8 minutes, then drain. Cook the tagliolini in a large pan of lightly salted, boiling water according to the package instructions, until tender. Drain well.

3 Heat the oil in a large skillet, add the asparagus, and stir gently to coat. Season to taste with salt and pepper and add the lemon juice.

4 Add the lemon rind and the tagliolini and heat through, tossing frequently, then add the smoked salmon. Transfer to warm bowls and serve immediately.

Cod

on a Bed of Vegetables

In the **best** company: White-fleshed, low-fat cod simmers in
aromatic juices under a cover of **crispy,** cooked vegetables

Ingredients

5–6 shallots

1¼ pounds **potatoes** · 2 **carrots**

3½ ounces **celery root** · 1 **leek**

4 **tomatoes**

2 tablespoons **butter**

salt · **pepper**

1 **garlic clove** · 2 **bay leaves**

½ cup **dry white wine**

1¾ cups **fish stock**

2¾ pounds **cod fillet**

1 **lemon**

½ bunch of fresh **parsley**

566 kcal, 9 g fat

Preparation
SERVES 4

1 Peel the shallots, potatoes, carrots, and celery root. Trim the
leek, cut in half lengthwise, and rinse. Slice the shallots in half
and cut the remaining vegetables into bitesize pieces.

2 Place the tomatoes in a bowl, pour in boiling water to cover, and
let stand for 2 minutes, then drain, and peel. Cut into fourths
and remove the seeds. Melt the butter in a large skillet and cook
the vegetables until softened. Season with salt and pepper.
Peel and finely chop the garlic, then add to the skillet with the
bay leaves. Pour in the wine and fish stock.

3 Wash the cod, pat dry with paper towels, and rub with salt
and pepper. Squeeze the lemon and sprinkle the juice over the
fish. Place the fish in the skillet and spoon the vegetables over it.
Cover and cook gently over medium heat for 35–40 minutes.

4 Wash the parsley and shake dry, then pull off the leaves, and
chop finely. Sprinkle over the fish and serve immediately with
boiled potatoes or white bread if you like.

**This cooking method is also ideal for other
types of firm-fleshed fish that keep their shape
and texture during cooking. Try using haddock,
monkfish, red snapper, mahi-mahi, or even
swordfish.**

Monkfish
on Red Lentils

Two on the same wavelength: The delicate broiled fish fillet is a delightful companion to the elegant combination of lentils and leeks

Ingredients

1¾ pounds **leeks**

about 2 tablespoons **oil**

scant 1 cup **red lentils**

1¾ cups **vegetable** or

fish stock

1¼ pounds **monkfish fillet**

white pepper

2 tablespoons **lime juice**

1 tablespoon **balsamic vinegar**

sea salt

3 tablespoons chopped fresh

tarragon or **parsley leaves**

460 kcal, 10 g fat

Preparation
SERVES 4

1 Trim and rinse the leeks, then cut into short, thin strips. Heat 1 tablespoon of the oil in a shallow pan and cook the leeks over medium heat, stirring occasionally, until softened. Add the lentils and stock, bring to a boil, then cover, and simmer gently for 5–8 minutes, until the lentils are just soft.

2 Meanwhile, preheat the broiler and oil the rack. Wash the fish fillet, pat dry with paper towels, and cut into four equal pieces. Season with pepper and lime juice. Broil the fish for about 4 minutes on each side, until tender and cooked through.

3 Season the lentil mixture with balsamic vinegar, salt, and pepper, and stir in 2 tablespoons of the herbs. Transfer to a serving dish.

4 Lightly season the fish fillets with salt, arrange them on the lentils, and sprinkle over the remaining herbs. Garnish with halved lime slices if you like.

Fine red lentils, which are particularly flavorful, are peeled and halved. Unlike most other legumes, they do not need soaking. They will disintegrate if cooked for too long.

Catfish Fillet
on Kohlrabi Vegetables

Preparation

1 Rinse the fish fillets and pat dry with paper towels. Season with salt and pepper and sprinkle over the lemon juice.

2 Peel and dice the kohlrabi. Melt half the butter and cook the kohlrabi until softened. Add the wine and simmer gently until slightly reduced. Season with salt and pepper, pour in the stock, cover, and simmer gently for about 10 minutes.

3 Melt the remaining butter in a skillet and cook the fish fillets for about 3 minutes on each side.

4 Combine the cornstarch with 1 tablespoon water and mix to a smooth paste. Stir into the sauce, bring to a boil, then add the vermouth. Combine the yoghurt and sour cream and add to the sauce.

5 Rinse the arugula and pat dry. Arrange the fish and kohlrabi mixture on individual plates, garnish with the arugula, and serve. Boiled potatoes or rice would go very well with this dish.

42

Ingredients

4 **catfish fillets** (each about 5½ ounces)

salt · pepper

1 tablespoon **lemon juice**

14 ounces **kohlrabi** · 2 tablespoons **butter**

½ cup **dry white wine**

1¼ cups **vegetable stock**

1 tablespoon **cornstarch**

3 tablespoons **dry vermouth**

3 tablespoons **plain yoghurt**

3 tablespoons **sour cream**

½ bunch of **arugula**

>> **261 kcal, 11 g fat**

Ingredients

2 carrots · 1 leek

5 ounces **Chinese cabbage**

5 ounces **Savoy cabbage**

4 tablespoons **bean sprouts**

1½ pounds **cod fillet**

2 tablespoons **lemon juice** · **salt** · **pepper**

1 tablespoon **rice flour**

3 **shallots** · 2 tablespoons **oil**

2 **lemongrass stalks**

scant 1 cup **fish stock**

1 **garlic clove** · 1 boiled **potato**

▶▶ **260 kcal, 7 g fat**

Crispy Cod
from the Wok

Preparation
SERVES 4

1 Peel the carrots, rinse the leeks and cabbage, and slice them all into thin strips. Rinse the bean sprouts and drain. Cut the fish into bitesize pieces and sprinkle with lemon juice. Season with salt and pepper, then coat with the rice flour. Trim and chop the shallots.

2 Heat the oil in a wok and cook the fish on both sides until crisp, then remove and keep warm. Cook the shallots in the oil until translucent, then add the vegetables, and stir-fry. Cut off the white pieces of the lemongrass and flatten with the blade of a heavy knife. Add to the wok and pour in the fish stock. Peel the garlic and crush it into the wok, then simmer gently for about 3 minutes. Remove the lemongrass from the sauce.

3 Press the potato through a ricer and stir into the sauce with a balloon whisk, then season with salt and pepper. Put the fish in the sauce and heat through, then serve.

Fillet of Perch
in Leek and Saffron Sauce

Three cheers for the Alps: This tasty freshwater fish is given a cosmopolitan twist in this Swiss recipe

Ingredients

2 leeks · salt

¼ cup **dry white wine**

2 tablespoons **dry vermouth**

½ cup **vegetable stock**

scant ½ cup **crème fraîche**

or **sour cream**

pinch of **saffron powder**

about 1¼ pounds **perch fillets**

2 tablespoons **oil**

saffron threads · fresh **dill sprigs**

262 kcal, 13 g fat

Preparation
SERVES 4

1 Trim, rinse, and slice the leeks. Blanch in boiling salted water for about 4 minutes, then tip into a strainer, rinse under cold running water, and drain well.

2 Bring the wine and vermouth to a boil in a pan and continue to boil until reduced by about half. Add the stock, crème fraîche, saffron powder, and leeks, lower the heat, and simmer gently for about 2 minutes, then set aside, and keep warm.

3 Rinse the fish and pat dry with paper towels. Season with salt and pepper. Heat the oil in a large skillet and cook the fillets on both sides over medium heat.

4 Place the leeks and saffron sauce on warm plates, arrange the fish on top of the sauce, and serve garnished with saffron threads and dill sprigs. Rice or ribbon pasta would go well with this dish.

Perch is widely found in lakes and rivers throughout the United States, but is not often seen in supermarkets. If you don't know a friendly fisherman, substitute any firm-fleshed fish.

Pork Tenderloin
with Fruity Rice

Now for something exotic: Based on Creole specialties, this culinary

offering consists of delicate pork medallions and fruit rice

Ingredients

3 scallions · 2 tablespoons oil

1 cup long grain rice

1¾ cups vegetable stock

1¼ pounds pork tenderloin

2 tablespoons clarified butter

1 small papaya

1 small pineapple · 1 tomato

salt · pepper

3 tablespoons dry sherry

⅔ cup sour cream

grated rind and juice of

1 lime

558 kcal, 17 g fat

Preparation
SERVES 4

1 Trim, rinse, and slice the scallions. Heat the oil in a large pan, add the rice, and cook, stirring constantly, for 1–2 minutes, until the grains are coated. Pour in the stock and bring to a boil. Cover and simmer gently for 20 minutes.

2 Wipe the pork tenderloin with paper towels. Melt the clarified butter in a skillet and cook the pork over medium heat until golden brown on both sides. Lower the heat, cover, and cook for 8–10 minutes more.

3 Peel the papaya, cut in half lengthwise, and remove the seeds, then cut the flesh into chunks. Cut off the pineapple top and peel. Cut the flesh into slices, then into bitesize pieces, discarding the core. Rinse and dice the tomato. Add the fruit and tomato to the cooked rice.

4 Remove the meat from the skillet, season with salt and pepper, wrap in foil, and leave to rest. Drain off the fat from the skillet. Stir the sherry and sour cream into the juices in the skillet over low heat. Season with salt, pepper, and lime juice. Slice the pork. Season the fruit rice with salt, pepper, grated lime rind, and lime juice. Arrange the rice, meat, and sauce on plates and serve.

To reduce the fat content even more, poach the pork tenderloin: Bring about 4 cups vegetable stock to a boil, place the tenderloin in the stock, and simmer gently for 10–12 minutes.

Chicken
with Orange-Flavored Vegetables

Based on a real classic: Inspired by sumptuous duck à l'orange,
this is a light version with Asian spices

Ingredients

4 skinless, boneless

chicken breast portions

salt · white pepper · 4 oranges

½ cup dry white wine

½ teaspoon ground coriander

14 ounces carrots

2 celery stalks

1 onion · 3 tablespoons oil

½ cup chicken stock

1 teaspoon lemon juice

ground star anise

ground cinnamon

sugar · 2 teaspoons maple syrup

½ bunch of fresh parsley

▶▶ 300 kcal, 7 g fat

Preparation
SERVES 4

1 Rinse the chicken and pat dry with paper towels. Season with salt and pepper. Squeeze the juice from one of the oranges. Combine the orange juice, 2 tablespoons of the wine, and the coriander in a shallow dish. Add the chicken and marinate for about 20 minutes.

2 Meanwhile, peel and dice the carrots. Trim, rinse, and thinly slice the celery. Peel and finely chop the onion. Heat half the oil in a pan and cook the onion until softened. Add the carrots and celery and cook for a few minutes more. Add the stock, the remaining wine, the lemon juice, star anise, cinnamon, and sugar. Cover simmer over low heat for 15 minutes.

3 Drain the chicken. Heat the remaining oil in a skillet and cook the chicken on both sides over medium heat until golden. Brush with the maple syrup and cook, turning frequently, for 10 minutes more.

4 Peel the remaining oranges, then cut out the segments from the membranes over a bowl to catch the juice. Rinse the parsley and shake dry, then pull off the leaves, and chop. Add the orange segments, juice, and parsley to the vegetables and heat through, then check the seasoning. Slice the meat diagonally and arrange on serving plates with the vegetables.

For a finishing touch, sprinkle a few walnut halves over the chicken and vegetables, and garnish with thinly pared orange rind. Use an unwaxed or thoroughly washed orange.

48

Braised Chicken
with Mushrooms and Vegetables

Preparation
SERVES 4

1 Trim and wipe the mushrooms, then chop. Peel and rinse the vegetables, as appropriate, then chop coarsely.

2 Cut the chicken into four pieces and rub them all over with salt and pepper. Heat the oil in a heavy skillet and cook over high heat until golden brown all over. Remove from the skillet and set aside.

3 Stir-fry the shallots, garlic, celery, and carrots briefly, then add the Jerusalem artichokes and the potatoes, and cook briefly. Pour over the wine, bring to a boil, and then simmer gently over low heat.

4 Put the chicken in the pan with the stock, then add the bay leaves, and season to taste with salt and pepper. Stir in the thyme. Cover and simmer gently over low heat for 5 minutes. Add the peas, then the mushrooms and continue to simmer until the chicken is tender and cooked through. Arrange the chicken pieces on a dish with the vegetables. Garnish with dill sprigs if you like.

50

Ingredients

1 cup mixed **exotic mushrooms**

10 **shallots** · 4 **garlic cloves**

3 **celery stalks** · 2 **carrots**

3½ ounces **Jerusalem artichokes**

7 ounces small **potatoes**

2¼-pound **chicken**

salt · **pepper**

1 tablespoon **oil** · ⅔ cup **dry white wine**

2¼ cups **vegetable stock** · 2 **bay leaves**

1 teaspoon dried **thyme**

½ cup **peas** (frozen)

435 kcal, 20 g fat

Ingredients

1 **garlic bulb**

1 pound 10 ounces **beef tenderloin**

salt · pepper

1 tablespoon **clarified butter**

1 **shallot** · 1 tablespoon **olive oil**

1 tablespoon **tomato paste**

14-ounce can **peeled tomatoes**

(8½ ounces drained weight)

sugar · Tabasco sauce

lemon wedges

▶▶ **280 kcal, 10 g fat**

Beef Tenderloin
with Tomato Sauce

Preparation
SERVES 4

1 Preheat the oven to 400°F. Divide the garlic into cloves, but do not peel.

2 Rub the beef with salt and pepper. Melt the clarified butter in a skillet and cook the meat over high heat until browned all over. Place the beef in a roasting pan with the garlic cloves and roast in the middle of the oven for about 25 minutes. Then turn the oven off, open the door, and leave the meat in the oven to rest.

3 To make the tomato sauce, peel and finely chop the shallot. Heat the oil in a skillet and cook until translucent. Stir in the tomato paste and the tomatoes, with their can juice. Break up the tomatoes slightly with a fork, then season with salt, pepper, sugar, and a dash of Tabasco. Simmer, uncovered, for about 10 minutes.

4 Slice the beef, arrange on a serving dish with the garlic and tomato sauce, and garnish with lemon wedges.

Veal Shank
with Carrots and Leeks

Everything comes to him who waits: Braised dishes call for patience—
and the reward is a soft-as-butter, juicy piece of meat

Ingredients

1 onion · 11 ounces **carrots**

14 ounces **leeks**

4 **veal shank slices**

(about 5 ounces each)

salt · pepper · 2 tablespoons **oil**

scant ½ cup **white wine**

2¼ cups **vegetable stock**

2 teaspoons **cornstarch**

¼ cup **crème fraîche**

or **sour cream**

346 kcal, 17 g fat

Preparation
SERVES 4

1 Peel and finely chop the onion. Peel the carrots and cut into small pieces. Trim and rinse the leeks and cut into strips.

2 Season the veal with salt and pepper. Heat the oil in a large pan and brown the meat on all sides. Add the onion and cook for 2–3 minutes, until softened. Pour in the stock and wine, cover, and simmer gently over low heat for about 1 hour.

3 Add the carrots, re-cover, and simmer for 10 minutes more. Combine the cornstarch with 2 tablespoons water in a small bowl and stir to a smooth paste, then stir into the sauce.

4 Add the leeks, bring back to a boil, then remove the pan from the heat. Stir in the crème fraîche. Taste and adjust the seasoning if necessary. Garnish with fresh thyme sprigs, if you like, and serve with boiled potatoes.

This dish is an Austrian specialty. The veal becomes wonderfully tender after long, slow cooking. This is the same cut of veal as that used for osso buco, and is sometimes sold under that name.

Veal Roulades
with Spinach and Mozzarella

Preparation
SERVES 4

1 Wash the spinach and cook in salted, boiling water for 5 minutes. Drain thoroughly. Place the scallops between two sheets of plastic wrap and beat with a rolling pin or the flat side of a meat mallet to flatten. Peel and crush the garlic. Spread the garlic over the scallops and season with salt and pepper. Place the slices of ham on top.

2 Squeeze out the moisture from the spinach, then separate it with your fingers, and arrange on the scallops. Dice the mozzarella and sprinkle over the spinach. Roll up the scallops and secure the rolls with toothpicks. Coat the roulades in the flour, shaking off any excess.

3 Heat the butter and the oil in a skillet and cook the roulades for about 5 minutes until browned all over. Gradually pour in the stock, then cover, and simmer gently over low heat for about 20 minutes.

4 Arrange the roulades with the sauce. Serve garnished with sliced tomatoes and fresh basil leaves if you like.

54

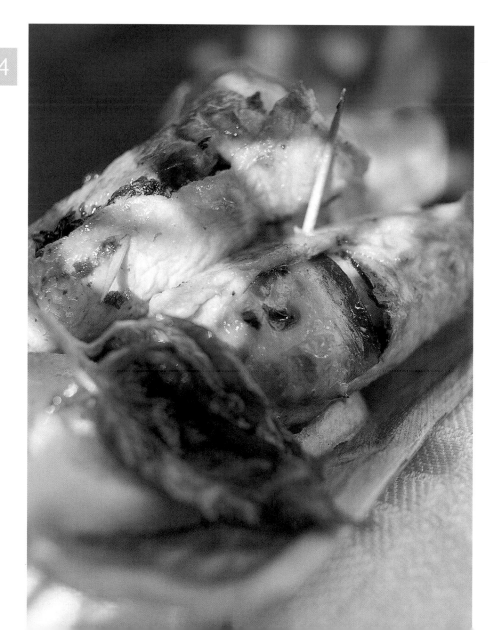

Ingredients

12 ounces **leaf spinach** · **salt**

8 small thin **veal scallops**

2–3 **garlic cloves** · **pepper**

8 thin slices **Parma ham**

4 ounces **mozzarella cheese**

2 tablespoons **all-purpose flour**

1 tablespoon **butter**

1 tablespoon **olive oil**

1¾ cups **vegetable stock**

315 kcal, 13 g fat

Ingredients

2 boned **saddles of rabbit**

(about 1¾ pounds)

salt · pepper

1 tablespoon **all-purpose flour**

1¼ pounds small **onions**

4 **garlic cloves** · 2 tablespoons **olive oil**

1 cup **red wine** · 2 **bay leaves**

1 **cinnamon stick** · 3 **cloves**

½ teaspoon dried **thyme**

1¼ pounds **tomatoes**

1 tablespoon **red wine vinegar**

2 tablespoons chopped fresh **thyme**

▶▶ **353 kcal, 8 g fat**

Stifado of Rabbit
with Thyme

Preparation
SERVES 4

1 Cut the meat into 2-inch slices. Season with salt and pepper and sprinkle with flour. Peel the onions and cut into fourths. Peel and thinly slice the garlic.

2 Heat the oil in a skillet and cook the slices of meat on both sides, then remove from the skillet, and keep warm. Add the onions and garlic to the skillet and cook until softened. Return the meat to the skillet, pour in half the wine, and add the bay leaves, cinnamon, cloves, and dried thyme. Cover and simmer gently over low heat for about 1 hour, gradually adding the remaining the wine.

3 Place the tomatoes in a bowl, cover with boiling water, and let stand for 2 minutes. Drain and peel off the skins, then cut in half, removing the seeds. Dice the flesh. Add the tomatoes to the skillet, re-cover, and simmer for 30 minutes more. Season with vinegar, salt, and pepper and sprinkle with fresh thyme before serving.

Lamb Chops
with Seasoned Butter

Mediterranean pleasures: The aroma of broiled meat and
fresh herbs creates a vacation atmosphere in the **kitchen**

Ingredients

12 lamb rib chops

salt · pepper

½-inch piece of fresh **ginger root**

2 **cardamom pods** · 2 **red chiles**

½ teaspoon **allspice berries**

½ teaspoon **ground cinnamon**

freshly grated **nutmeg**

2 tablespoons **clarified butter**

2 tablespoons **walnut oil**

2 **garlic cloves**

2 tablespoons chopped
fresh **parsley**

1 tablespoon chopped fresh **mint**

240 kcal, 14 g fat

Preparation
SERVES 4

1 Wash the lamb, pat dry with paper towels, and cut out the bones. Cut off the visible fat, then season the meat with salt and pepper. Peel and finely grate the ginger. Split open the cardamom pods and grind the seeds with the chiles and allspice in a mortar with a pestle. Combine with the ground cinnamon and nutmeg.

2 Heat the clarified butter and walnut oil in a small pan. Peel and crush the garlic into the pan. Stir in the spice mix and let it bubble up briefly. Stir in the parsley and mint, then remove the pan from the heat, and let cool slightly. Spread both sides of the lamb chops with the seasoned butter, reserving the remainder.

3 Heat a ridged griddle pan or heavy skillet. The chops can also be cooked on the barbecue. Cook over high heat, turning once, for 6–8 minutes, until well browned on the outside but still slightly pink in the center. Meanwhile, reheat the remaining butter. Arrange the chops on warm plates and pour over the seasoned butter. Garnish with parsley and lemon wedges if you like and serve with rice.

**Spinach tzatziki goes well with this dish:
Combine 5 ounces blanched, coarsely chopped
leaf spinach with ⅔ cup farmer's cheese,
⅔ cup plain yogurt, and 1 tablespoon lemon
juice. Season with salt and ground cinnamon.**

Vegetarian

Paprika Vegetables
with Cream Sauce

Enjoy the lightness: A brightly colored potpourri of vegetables,
enhanced by a light, creamy-smooth sauce

Ingredients

2 small **fennel bulbs**

2 **red bell peppers** · 2 **carrots**

2 large **potatoes** · 1 **leek**

2 **shallots**

2 tablespoons **butter**

3½ cups **vegetable stock** · 1 **lemon**

2 tablespoons **crème fraîche**

or **sour cream**

½ teaspoon **paprika**

2 tablespoons **light cream**

salt · **pepper**

250 kcal, 11 g fat

Preparation
SERVES 4

1 Trim and rinse the fennel. Cut in half lengthwise and then crosswise into thin strips. Cut the bell peppers in half lengthwise, seed, then rinse, and dice the flesh.

2 Peel the carrots and cut into long, thin strips. Peel and dice the potatoes. Trim the leek, cut in half lengthwise, rinse thoroughly, and slice crosswise. Peel and halve the shallots lengthwise, then slice crosswise.

3 Melt the butter in a large skillet. Add all the vegetables and cook over medium heat, stirring occasionally, for about 5 minutes. Pour in the stock, cover, and simmer for 10 minutes.

4 Wash the lemon in hot water, dry, and grate about 2 teaspoons rind. Stir the lemon rind, crème fraîche, paprika, and cream into the vegetables, then season well with salt and pepper, and serve.

Braising is probably the best cooking method for retaining flavor. Because the cooking liquid contains vitamins and minerals from the food after cooking, do use it as well.

Pumpkin Risotto
with Sage

Preparation
SERVES 4

1 Preheat the oven to 350°F. Cut the top off one pumpkin. Scoop out the flesh and seeds with a spoon, taking care not to damage the outer shell. Peel the second pumpkin. Remove the seeds and chop all the pumpkin flesh.

2 Wrap the pumpkin shell in foil and bake for 30 minutes. Peel and finely chop the onion. Melt 1 tablespoon of the butter in a pan and cook the onion until softened. Add the rice and cook, stirring constantly, until the grains are coated and shiny. Gradually add the hot stock, a ladleful at a time, stirring constantly. Make sure that all the stock has been absorbed before adding the next ladleful. The rice will be cooked when it has absorbed all the stock; this will take about 30 minutes. Add the pumpkin 10 minutes before the end of the cooking time.

3 Before serving, stir the remaining butter and the Parmesan into the risotto and season well with salt and pepper. Serve the rice in the pumpkin shell and garnish with sage leaves.

Ingredients

2 **pumpkins** (each about 1¾ pounds)

1 **onion**

2 tablespoons **butter**

2¾ cups **risotto rice** (arborio or Vialone)

1 cup hot **vegetable stock**

½ cup freshly grated **Parmesan cheese**

salt · pepper

fresh **sage leaves**, to garnish

400 kcal, 9 g fat

Ingredients

4 **onions**

2 tablespoons **butter**

2 tablespoons **Madeira**

2 tablespoons **raisins**

3–4 fresh **sage sprigs**

2 tablespoons **pine nuts**

2–3 tablespoons **bread crumbs**

4–5 tablespoons **vegetable stock**

▶▶ **180 kcal, 8 g fat**

Stuffed Onions
with Pine Nuts and Raisins

Preparation
SERVES 4

1 Peel the onions and cook in lightly salted, boiling water for about 15 minutes. Drain well and cool slightly. Cut the top off each onion, and scoop out some of the flesh from the lower portions with a teaspoon.

2 Finely chop the scooped-out flesh. Melt 1 tablespoon of the butter in a skillet and cook the chopped onion, until translucent. Add the Madeira and raisins and simmer for a few minutes. Preheat the oven to 350°F.

3 Wash the sage and shake dry. Pull off the leaves from the stalks and chop finely. Roast the pine nuts in a dry, nonstick skillet. Add to the cooked onion with the bread crumbs and the chopped sage, mix thoroughly then spoon into the onion shells.

4 Place the onions in a lightly oiled ovenproof dish. Top with the "lids" and pour over the stock. Dot with small pieces of butter and bake for 45 minutes.

Polenta
with a Vegetable Crust

Best wishes from Italy: Golden yellow cornmeal with fresh vegetables and aromatic herbs guarantee culinary pleasure that is bursting with summer freshness

Ingredients

2 tablespoons **olive oil**

¼ teaspoon each fresh **thyme**

and **oregano**

2¼ cups **vegetable stock**

generous 1 cup **polenta**

1 **onion** · 2 **garlic cloves**

1 **red bell pepper**

½ teaspoon **paprika** (sweet)

cayenne pepper · **salt** · **pepper**

3¼ ounces **Fontina**, **Taleggio**,

or **Swiss cheese**

1 **lemon**

2 tablespoons each chopped

fresh **parsley** and **rosemary**

14 ounces **zucchini**

289 kcal, 9 g fat

Preparation
SERVES 4

1 Heat 1 tablespoon of the olive oil in a pan and briefly cook the thyme and oregano. Pour in the stock and stir in the polenta. Cook for 3 minutes, then turn off the heat, and let stand for about 10 minutes. Spread out the polenta evenly in a lightly oiled ovenproof dish.

2 Peel and finely chop the onion and garlic. Cut the bell pepper in half lengthwise, seed, then rinse, and finely chop the flesh.

3 Heat the remaining oil in a skillet and cook the onion, garlic, and bell pepper, stirring occasionally, until softened. Season well with paprika, cayenne, salt, and pepper. Preheat the oven to 400°F.

4 Coarsely grate the cheese. Wash the lemon in hot water, dry, and grate the rind finely. Gently stir the grated lemon rind, cheese, parsley, and rosemary into the paprika vegetables. Squeeze the juice from the lemon.

5 Trim and rinse the zucchini and cut into very thin strips. Season with 1–2 tablespoons lemon juice and salt and spread over the polenta. Top the zucchini with the paprika vegetables. Bake the polenta for 20–25 minutes, until crisp.

Tomato Lentils
on Ribbon Pasta

Minimum effort for maximum effect: A clever sugo, or sauce,
made from tomatoes, red wine, and lentils that everyone will enjoy!

Ingredients

1 onion · 2 garlic cloves

1 bunch of green soup vegetables

2 tablespoons butter

⅔ cup green lentils

2 large cans tomatoes

(1¼ pounds drained weight)

½ cup red wine · 1 bay leaf

1 fresh thyme sprig · sugar

salt · pepper

1¼ pounds ribbon pasta

½ bunch of fresh parsley

665 kcal, 7 g fat

Preparation
SERVES 4

1 Peel and finely chop the onion and garlic. If necessary, cut the green soup vegetables into small pieces.

2 Melt the butter in a skillet and cook the onion, garlic, vegetables, and lentils, stirring constantly, until the onion is softened and translucent.

3 Add the tomatoes, with their can juices, red wine, bay leaf, and thyme. Season with a little sugar, salt, and pepper. Bring to a boil, then cover, and simmer over medium heat for about 25 minutes, until the lentils are soft.

4 Cook the pasta in a large pan of lightly salted, boiling water according to the package instructions, then drain.

5 Wash the parsley and shake dry. Pull off the leaves from the stalks and chop finely. Remove and discard the bay leaf and thyme from the tomato sauce. Season the sauce with salt and pepper, then stir in the parsley. Toss the tomato and lentils with the pasta in a serving dish. Garnish with more fresh thyme and parsley before serving if you like.

Lentils are one of the oldest cultivated plants, and are a staple food in many countries. Green lentils—especially the slightly more expensive, dark green Puy lentils—are among the tastiest.

Baked Eggplant
with Spaghetti

Preparation
SERVES 4

1 Trim and rinse the eggplant and cut diagonally into eight ¾-inch thick slices. Sprinkle with lemon juice and herb salt. Wrap the eggplant slices in foil and set aside for about 30 minutes.

2 Preheat the oven to 350°F. Finely dice the cheese with a sharp knife. Peel and finely chop the onion and garlic. Wash the herbs and shake dry, then finely chop the leaves, and combine with the onion, garlic, and cheese.

3 Dry the eggplant slices with paper towels, then season with pepper, and place in a single layer in a lightly oiled, ovenproof dish. Rinse the tomatoes, then cut each into four slices, and place on top of the eggplant. Cover with the cheese and herb mixture and bake for about 25–30 minutes.

4 Meanwhile, cook the spaghetti in a large pan of lightly salted, boiling salted water according to the package instructions. Drain, toss with the eggplant, and serve.

Ingredients

1 large **eggplant** (about 1¼ pounds)

1 teaspoon **lemon juice**

½ teaspoon **herb salt**

3 ounces **Swiss cheese**

1 small **onion** · 2 **garlic cloves**

2 sprigs each fresh **basil** and **oregano**

pepper · 2 **tomatoes**

11 ounces **spaghetti** · **salt**

380 kcal, 8 g fat

Ingredients

5 cups **orecchiette** · **salt**

pepper

1¼ pounds **broccoli**

4 **garlic cloves**

2 fresh **red chiles**

4 tablespoons **olive oil**

½ cup freshly grated

Parmesan cheese

▶▶ **555 kcal, 9 g fat**

69

Pasta Shells
with Broccoli

Preparation
SERVES 4

1 Cook the orecchiette in a large pan of lightly salted, boiling water according to the package instructions, then drain well.

2 Trim and rinse the broccoli and cut into small flowerets. Blanch the flowerets in lightly salted, boiling water for about 4 minutes. Drain, then combine with the cooked orecchiette, and set aside until required.

3 Peel and finely chop the garlic. Cut the chiles in half lengthwise, seed, then rinse, and chop the flesh into small pieces. Heat the olive oil in the pasta pan with the garlic and chiles. Toss the orecchiette and broccoli flowerets in the oil, and season with salt and pepper.

4 Arrange the orecchiette on warm plates and sprinkle with Parmesan before serving.

Baked Ratatouille
with Herbs

Colorful and healthy: A Mediterranean mixture of vegetables
with herbes de Provence stirs memories of culinary treats on vacation

Ingredients

2 each small **red** and **green**

bell peppers

1 small **zucchini** · 1 **eggplant**

1 **onion** · 14 ounces **tomatoes**

4 **garlic cloves**

3 tablespoons **olive oil**

salt · **pepper**

1½ tablespoons dried

herbes de Provence

2 tablespoons **lemon juice**

1 cup **vegetable stock**

▸▸ **121 kcal, 4 g fat**

Preparation
SERVES 4

1 Preheat the oven to 425°F. Cut the bell peppers in half lengthwise, seed, rinse, and slice the halves lengthwise. Trim and rinse the zucchini and eggplant. Cut the zucchini into thin strips and the eggplant into coarse chunks.

2 Peel the onion and slice lengthwise. Rinse the tomatoes, then cut into fourths. Remove the seeds and chop the flesh. Peel and finely chop the garlic.

3 Brush an ovenproof dish with a little olive oil and place the prepared vegetables in it. Season well with salt and pepper and sprinkle with the herbs. Sprinkle over the remaining oil and the lemon juice and pour in the stock.

4 Bake the ratatouille for about 30 minutes, turning once. Garnish with fresh rosemary sprigs before serving if you like.

If you have only ever had ratatouille cooked on the stovetop, you really should try this version. The juices that are created during the roasting process provide a more intensive aroma.

Broiled Vegetables
with Basmati Rice

Hot favorites: Even non-vegetarians are unable to
resist zucchini, onions, and tomatoes served straight from the broiler

Ingredients

½ cup **basmati rice**

salt · 1 green **zucchini**

2 yellow **zucchini**

2 red **onions**

1¼ pounds **cherry tomatoes**

1 tablespoon fresh **rosemary**

bunch of fresh **parsley**

pepper

juice of 1 **lemon**

4 tablespoons **olive oil**

1 tablespoon **butter**

177 kcal, 4 g fat

Preparation
SERVES 4

1 Wash the rice thoroughly in a strainer under cold running water until the water runs clear, then place in a pan with 1 cup lightly salted water, and bring to a boil. Lower the heat, cover, and simmer gently for about 20 minutes.

2 Trim and rinse the zucchini. Depending on their size, halve or slice them. Peel the onions and cut each into eight wedges. Rinse and dry the cherry tomatoes. Finely chop the rosemary. Rinse the parsley and shake dry, then pull off the leaves from the stalks, and chop them finely.

3 Preheat the broiler. Cook the vegetables for about 10 minutes, making sure that the heat is not too high. While they are cooking, drizzle with lemon juice, season with salt and pepper, brush with olive oil, and sprinkle over the rosemary. Alternatively, cook the vegetables on a barbecue.

4 Just before serving stir the butter and chopped parsley into the rice and arrange on plates with the broiled vegetables.

Many types of vegetable are suitable for broiling, especially firm ones, such as carrots, bell peppers, and fennel. The vegetables can also be cut into pieces and threaded onto skewers.

Baked Potatoes
with Sour Cream Dip

Preparation
SERVES 4

1 Preheat the oven to 400°F. Scrub the potatoes with a vegetable brush under cold running water.

2 Wrap each potato in aluminum foil (shiny side inside) and bake on a shelf in the oven for 1–1½ hours, until tender when gently squeezed.

3 Meanwhile, combine the sour cream and yogurt in a bowl and stir until smooth. Wash the parsley and shake dry, pull off the leaves from the stalks, and chop finely.

Stir the parsley into the sour cream mixture and season with salt, a little sugar, and pepper.

4 Remove the potatoes from the oven. Open the foil parcels, but do not remove the potatoes completely. With a sharp knife, cut a large X-shape into the top of each potato and gently squeeze open. Spoon a little of the sour cream dip into each potato and serve the remainder separately in a bowl. A mixed salad would go well with the potatoes.

Ingredients

8 large **baking potatoes**

½ cup **sour cream**

scant 1 cup **whole milk plain yogurt**

½ bunch of fresh **parsley**

salt · sugar

pepper

297 kcal, 7 g fat

Ingredients

2 **red bell peppers**

1¼ pounds firm **bean curd**

12 **scallions**

3⅔ cups small **mushrooms**

1 **garlic clove**

1 fresh **thyme sprig**

4 tablespoons **olive oil**

paprika

pepper

▶▶ **185 kcal, 8 g fat**

Vegetable Skewers
with Bean Curd

Preparation
SERVES 4

1 Preheat the broiler. These skewers can also be cooked on the barbecue—light it about 30 minutes before you plan to cook them.

2 Cut the peppers in half lengthwise, seed, then rinse the halves. Cut each into ¾-inch squares. Using a sharp knife, slice the bean curd and then cut into 1½-inch squares. (A blunt knife will squash it.) Trim, rinse, and slice the scallions and mushrooms.

3 Alternately thread the vegetables, mushrooms, and bean curd slices onto presoaked wooden skewers. Peel and finely chop the garlic. Wash the thyme and pat dry, then pull off the leaves, and chop coarsely.

4 Make a paste from the olive oil, garlic, thyme, a little paprika, and pepper. Brush the skewers all over with the paste. Broil the skewers or cook on the barbecue for 5–8 minutes, until tender and beginning to char.

Pancake Wraps
with Asian Vegetables

An edible parcel: Freshly cooked pancakes keep the Asian vegetable
filling hot and they also provide a delicious accompaniment

Ingredients

3 eggs

2½ cups all-purpose flour · salt

1½ cups low-fat milk

about ⅔ cup mineral water

2 red bell peppers

1 small eggplant · 1 zucchini

2 cups oyster mushrooms

1 cup bean sprouts

1-inch piece of fresh ginger root

2 tablespoons oil · pepper

½ cup vegetable stock

2 tablespoons vinegar

1 tablespoon maple syrup

1 teaspoon cornstarch

2–3 tablespoons soy sauce

460 kcal, 13 g fat

Preparation
SERVES 4

1 To make the pancake batter, combine the eggs, flour, a little salt, and the milk and beat well. Add enough mineral water to make a thin batter. Cover and let stand for 30 minutes.

2 Meanwhile, rinse the bell peppers, eggplant, and zucchini and slice thinly, seeding the bell peppers. Trim the mushrooms and cut into fourths. Rinse the bean sprouts. Peel and chop the ginger.

3 Heat a little oil in a nonstick skillet. Add one-eighth of the batter and tip the skillet to coat the base. Cook for 2 minutes, or until the underside is golden, flip over, and cook the other side for 1 minute, until golden. Cook seven more pancakes in the same way. Stack, interleaved with wax paper, and keep warm.

4 Heat the remaining oil. Add the ginger and cook briefly, then add the eggplant and bell peppers, then the zucchini and mushrooms, and cook until softened. Season with salt and pepper. Add the stock, vinegar, and maple syrup. Combine the cornstarch with 1 tablespoon water and stir into the vegetables. Stir in the bean sprouts and soy sauce. Place some of the filling on one fourth of each pancake, then fold the sides over twice. Garnish with cilantro leaves before serving.

If you're short of time use ready-made tortillas that you just heat in a skillet or microwave oven instead of making your own pancakes. The wraps will still taste wonderful.

Vegetable Couscous
with a Tomato Dip

Ideal as an entrée in summer: This classic North African dish is combined with steamed vegetables and a spicy dip

Ingredients

6 tomatoes · 1 onion

3 garlic cloves · 1 tablespoon oil

⅔ cup creamy plain yogurt

salt · pepper · Tabasco sauce

sugar · 2⅓ cups couscous

2 zucchini · 3 carrots

1 eggplant · ⅔ cup green beans

3½ ounces white cabbage leaves

1 dried chile

2 tablespoons clarified butter

1 cup vegetable stock

generous ½ cup garbanzo beans

(canned)

pinch of saffron powder

565 kcal, 14 g fat

Preparation
SERVES 4

1 To make the tomato dip, rinse two of the tomatoes, cut into fourths, seed, then coarsely chop the flesh. Peel and finely chop the onion and one garlic clove. Heat the oil in a pan and cook the onion and garlic until translucent. Add the tomatoes and simmer gently over medium heat. Remove from the heat and process with a handheld blender until smooth. Add the yogurt, then season with salt, pepper, Tabasco, and sugar. Cover and cool, then chill.

2 Pour boiling water over the couscous in a bowl and set aside for 5 minutes. Fluff up with a fork and keep warm.

3 Trim and rinse the zucchini, then cut into thick strips. Rinse the remaining tomatoes, cut into fourths, seed, and finely chop the flesh. Peel and dice the carrots. Trim, rinse, and coarsely chop the eggplant. Trim and rinse the green beans and cut in half if necessary. Rinse and shred the cabbage. Peel and chop the remaining garlic. Crush the chile in a mortar with a pestle.

4 Melt the clarified butter in a large skillet and cook the carrots, beans, and cabbage for 4 minutes. Add the garlic and chile, then the zucchini and eggplant. Lower the heat, cover, and simmer gently for 4 minutes. Pour in the stock, stir in the tomatoes and garbanzo beans, and simmer for 5 minutes more. Season with salt, pepper, and saffron.

5 Pile the couscous onto plates and top with the vegetables. Garnish with parsley or cilantro leaves, if you like, and serve with the tomato dip.

Desserts

Yogurt Cream
with Citrus Fruit

Pure **freshness:** This homemade yogurt cream is far superior
to store-bought varieties, both in flavor and **vitamin** content

Ingredients

1 orange · 2 lemons

⅓ cup **sugar**

2¼ cups **whole milk plain yogurt**

2 tablespoons **orange liqueur**

(such as Cointreau)

1 **lime**

4 fresh **lemon balm sprigs**

195 kcal, 5 g fat

Preparation
SERVES 4

1 Peel the orange with a sharp knife, taking care to remove all the
bitter white pith. Cut out the orange segments from between the
membranes, working over a bowl to catch the juice, then squeeze
the juice from the membranes. Squeeze the lemons.

2 Place the sugar on a plate. Dip the rims of four sundae glasses in
the orange juice, then in the sugar to give them a sugary frosting.

3 Combine the yogurt, orange and lemon juice, orange liqueur, and
sugar in a bowl and beat with a whisk, then divide among the
dishes. Place the orange segments on top.

4 Wash the lime in hot water, then dry, and slice thinly. Wash the
lemon balm and pat dry with paper towels, then garnish the
dishes with slices of lime and lemon balm sprigs.

**To give the yogurt cream a little
additional color, you could use a blood
orange or a pink grapefruit. This
variation is particularly attractive
garnished with fresh mint leaves.**

Mixed Berries
with Buckwheat

Preparation
SERVES 4

1 Put the buckwheat in a large pan with 2¼ cups water and bring to a boil. Skim off the reddish foam that forms on the surface with a small strainer.

2 Lower the heat, then cover, and simmer gently for 20 minutes. Remove the pan from the heat and let stand for 15 minutes more.

3 Pick over the berries, then rinse, and drain thoroughly in a strainer. Choose some attractive currants or

strawberries with flowers or leaves attached to use for decoration and set aside.

4 Divide half the cooked buckwheat among four dishes, then divide the berries among them, and finally top with the remaining buckwheat.

5 Pour over the red currant juice and decorate with the reserved currants or berries. Sprinkle with confectioners' sugar before serving if you like.

Ingredients

1 cup **coarse buckwheat meal**

7 cups **mixed berries**

(such as red and black currants, blueberries,

strawberries, raspberries)

1¾ cups **red currant juice**

378 kcal, 1 g fat

Ingredients

4½ cups **mixed dried fruit**

(such as apricots, figs, prunes, dates)

scant ½ cup **golden raisins**

scant ¼ cup each skinned **almonds,**

pine nuts, and **pistachios**

3 tablespoons **sugar**

scant ½ cup **creamy plain yogurt**

▶▶ **334 kcal, 11 g fat**

Dried Fruit
with Nuts in Syrup

Preparation
SERVES 4

1 Place the dried fruit and golden raisins in a bowl, add warm water to cover, and let soak until plumped up. Drain well.

2 Place the dried fruit and golden raisins in a heavy pan with the almonds, pine nuts, and pistachios, sprinkle over the sugar, pour in 1 cup water, and stir well. Bring to a boil, then cover, and simmer gently over low heat for about 20 minutes.

3 Remove the pan from the heat and let the compote cool completely. Divide among four dessert bowls or glass dishes, cover with plastic wrap, and chill in the refrigerator for several hours.

4 To serve, stir the creamy yogurt until smooth and dot spoonfuls on top of the fruit. Alternatively fill a pastry bag with the yogurt and pipe swirls over the fruit. Decorate with little sprigs of fresh mint if you like.

Kiwi and Fig Salad
with Banana Topping

A touch of the exotic: This dessert pampers the palate with a refreshing
sharpness and the sweetness of sun-ripened fruits

Ingredients:

4 ripe **kiwi fruits**

4 fresh **green figs**

2 **apricots**

scant ½ cup **red currant juice**

1 tablespoon **almonds**

4 **dates**

1 **banana**

218 kcal, 2 g fat

Preparation
SERVES 4

1 Peel the kiwi fruits, then slice as thinly as possible, and arrange
them in a circle on four dessert plates. Rinse and dry the figs,
then cut each one into four or eight pieces and place on top
of the kiwi slices. Rinse the apricots, pit, and cut into thin strips.

2 Pour the juice into a pan, bring to a boil, then continue to boil
over high heat until thickened and syrupy. Coarsely chop the
almonds. Place the apricot strips in the red currant syrup and boil
briefly. Divide among the dessert plates, then top the fruit salad
with the chopped almonds.

3 Pit the dates and chop as finely as possible. Peel the banana and
mash with a fork. Combine the chopped dates with the banana.

4 Top the fruit salad with the banana and date mixture, then
decorate with fresh lemon balm if you like.

**Depending on season and availability,
you can, of course, use other fruits for
the fruit salad—perhaps tropical
varieties, such as mango, papaya, star
fruit, and pineapple.**

Semolina Flummery
with Strawberries

Preparation
SERVES 4

1 Bring the milk, vanilla extract, sugar, and a pinch of salt to a boil in a large pan. Sprinkle over the semolina and bring back to a boil, stirring constantly. Stir in the grated lemon rind and simmer for a few minutes. Remove the pan from the heat and let cool slightly.

2 Combine the egg yolk with a little of the hot semolina, then stir the mixture into the pan. Beat the egg whites until stiff and fold in. Rinse four soufflé dishes with cold water, then divide the mixture among them, and chill.

3 Meanwhile, rinse and hull the strawberries. Cut them in half or into fourths, depending on their size. Sprinkle over 1 tablespoon of the confectioners' sugar and let stand for at least 15 minutes.

4 Run a sharp knife around the inside of the dishes to loosen the desserts and invert them onto four serving plates. Decorate the flummeries with the strawberries and lemon balm sprigs. Sprinkle with the remaining confectioners' sugar before serving.

Ingredients

2¼ cups **low-fat milk**

1 teaspoon **vanilla extract**

½ cup **sugar · salt**

scant ½ cup **semolina**

grated rind of 1 **lemon**

1 **egg yolk**

2 **egg whites**

5 cups **strawberries**

2 tablespoons **confectioners' sugar**

fresh **lemon balm sprigs**

280 kcal, 5 g fat

Ingredients

2⅓ cups **raspberries**

8 **white gelatin leaves**

scant ½ cup **sugar**

1 tablespoon **vanilla sugar**

4 tablespoons **orange juice**

1 teaspoon grated **orange rind**

2⅔ cups **low-fat cream cheese**

5 teaspoons **raspberry liqueur**

⅔ cup **heavy cream**

▶▶ **330 kcal, 15 g fat**

Raspberry Cheesecakes
with Orange Syrup

Preparation
SERVES 4

1 Pick over the raspberries, then rinse them, and drain well. Soak the gelatin in a small, heatproof bowl of cold water.

2 Put the sugar, vanilla sugar, and 1 tablespoon water in a small pan and simmer for about 20 minutes, until syrupy.

3 Combine the sugar syrup, orange juice, and grated orange rind. Stir the cream cheese until smooth, then stir into the orange syrup. Add the raspberry liqueur.

4 Dissolve the gelatin over a pan of barely simmering water, then add to the cream cheese mixture in a steady stream, stirring constantly. Whip the cream until stiff and add to the cheese mixture with half the raspberries. Spoon into small molds and chill for 3 hours.

5 Dip the base of the molds in hot water, then invert onto plates. Top with the remaining raspberries. Cover with a glaze and decorate with fresh mint leaves if you like.

Grape Cup
with Coconut Cheese

Pleasure by the spoonful: Alternate layers of juicy pears and purple grapes, interspersed with creamy coconut cheese

Ingredients

7 ounces **purple grapes**

4 tablespoons **Crème de Cassis**

2 small **Williams pears**

1 tablespoon **lemon juice**

1 piece of freshly peeled **coconut**

(about 2 ounces)

scant 1 cup **cream cheese**

2 tablespoons **vanilla sugar**

fresh **mint leaves**

225 kcal, 8 g fat

Preparation
SERVES 4

1 Rinse the grapes, then halve, and seed if necessary. Combine the grapes and liqueur.

2 Rinse the pears, cut into fourths, then core, and cut crosswise into chunks. Sprinkle with the lemon juice and combine with the grapes. Finely grate two-thirds of the coconut.

3 Beat the cheese in a bowl with a whisk until creamy and smooth, then beat in the vanilla sugar and grated coconut.

4 Divide two-thirds of the fruit among four tall glasses. Spoon the coconut cheese over the fruit, then top with the remaining fruit. Use a vegetable peeler to shred the remaining coconut finely. Decorate the fruit cups with coconut strips and mint leaves.

If you want to serve this without adding alcohol—perhaps if you are serving it to children—then simply substitute black currant or red grape juice for the Crème de Cassis (black currant liqueur.)

Vanilla Ice Cream
with Fruit and Liqueur

A treat for those with a sweet tooth: Cream cheese and fruit combine to ensure that this fabulous ice melts in your mouth even without cream

Ingredients

2 vanilla beans

2½ cups low-fat cream cheese

2 tablespoons sugar

4 tablespoons advocaat

5 teaspoons Amaretto

1 cup each cherries
and raspberries

4 ice cream cones

fresh mint leaves

▶▶ 253 kcal, 2 g fat

Preparation
SERVES 4

1 Cut the vanilla beans open lengthwise and scoop out the seeds and pulp with a knife.

2 Combine the cream cheese, vanilla seeds and pulp, sugar, advocaat, and Amaretto in a freezerproof bowl. Freeze the mixture for at least 1 hour, beating well with a fork every 20 minutes. Alternatively, make the ice cream in an ice cream maker following the manufacturer's instructions.

3 Remove the stalks from the cherries. Rinse the cherries and raspberries and drain well.

4 To serve, put the fruit in the ice cream cones, reserving a few cherries to decorate. Scoop the ice cream into balls and place in the cones. Decorate the cones with the reserved cherries and the mint leaves.

If you do without the cones, you will save additional fat and calories. Freeze the ice in little soufflé molds, then invert onto plates, and decorate with the fruit before serving.

Muffins
with Cherries

Small but irresistibly good: Feather-light muffins,
full of sweet, juicy cherries—definitely not just for the children

Ingredients

scant 1 cup **sweet cherries**

(fresh or bottled)

1 **lime**

1⅔ cups **all-purpose flour**

1 teaspoon **baking powder**

⅔ cup soft **half-fat margarine**

¾ cup **sugar**

1 tablespoon **vanilla sugar**

1 **egg** · scant ½ cup **buttermilk**

confectioners' sugar, for sprinkling

▶▶ 173 kcal, 6 g fat

94

Preparation
MAKES 12

1 Preheat the oven to 350°F. If you are using fresh cherries, rinse
and pit them. Drain bottled cherries. Wash the lime in hot water
and dry. Finely grate the rind and squeeze out the juice.

2 Sift the flour and baking powder into a bowl. Beat together the
margarine, sugar, vanilla sugar, and egg in another bowl until
creamy. Fold in the grated lime rind, 2 tablespoons lime juice, and
the buttermilk. Add the flour mixture and combine quickly, then
add the cherries.

3 Spoon the mixture into nonstick muffin pans or paper cases,
filling them two-thirds full. Use two paper cases—one inside the
other—for each muffin. Bake 20–25 minutes, until golden.

4 Brush the muffins with the remaining lime juice while they are
still hot, then remove from the pans and place on a rack to cool.
Sprinkle lightly with confectioners' sugar before serving.

**If you use nonstick pans for baking, you
avoid the need to grease them before
adding the mixture. If your pans are not
nonstick, use paper cases instead to keep
the level of fat as low as possible.**

Index of Recipes

© Verlag Zabert Sandmann, Munich

Graphic design: Georg Feigl, Barbara Markwitz
Recipes: ZS team
Editors: Martina Solter, Kathrin Ullerich
Production: Karin Mayer, Peter Karg-Cordes
Lithography: inteca Media Service GmbH, Rosenheim
Print & Binding: Officine Grafiche De Agostini, Novara

English translation: Translate-A-Book, Oxford, UK
Typesetting: Organ Graphic, Abingdon, UK
Editing: Linda Doeser Publishing Services, London, UK

This edition published by Barnes & Noble, Inc.,
by arrangement with Zabert Sandmann.
2002 Barnes & Noble Books
M 11 10 9 8 7 6 5 4 3 2 1
Printed in Italy
ISBN: 0-7607-3720-7

Visit us also at our Internet website at www.zsverlag.de

Photo Credits

Cover photos: StockFood/S. & P. Eising (front and back)

Susie Eising: 29, 33, 54, 55, 57, 85; StockFood/Uwe Bender: 36; StockFood/Alexander van Berge: 58–59, 73; StockFood/Harry Bischof: 7 (bottom left), 13, 25, 42, 45, 53, 83; StockFood/Michael Brauner: 74; StockFood/Gerrit Buntrock: 69; StockFood/Jean Cazals: 37, 50, 62; StockFood/Brett Danton: 51; StockFood/Achim Deimling-Ostrinsky: 27; StockFood/Pete A. Eising: 79; StockFood/Susie Eising: 6 left, 8 (top right, bottom left, bottom right), 10–11, 17, 20, 35, 63, 75, 88, 89, 93; StockFood/S. & P. Eising: 1, 2–3, 4–5, 7 (top left, 2nd from bottom left, bottom center), 8 (top left), 14, 15, 19, 21, 23, 30–31, 39, 41, 47, 49, 61, 65, 67, 68, 71, 77, 80–81, 87, 91, 95; StockFood/Karl Newedel: 84; StockFood/Rosenfeld Images LTD: 6 right, 7 (top right); StockFood/Rosenfeld/Maximilian: 7 (2nd from top right); StockFood/Jan-Peter Westermann: 43